Best Little Houses

Best
Little
Houses

Introduction by Gale C. Steves,
Editor-in-Chief of HOME® Magazine

FRIEDMAN/FAIRFAX
PUBLISHERS

A FRIEDMAN/FAIRFAX BOOK

©1998 HOME® Magazine.

Library of Congress Cataloging-in-Publication data available upon request.

ISBN 1-56799-637-X

Special Thanks to Timothy Drew
Editor: Sharyn Rosart
Art Director: Jeff Batzli
Designer: Andrea Karman
Photography Editor: Amy Talluto
Production Director: Karen Matsu Greenberg
Floor Plan Illustrations: Steve Arcella
Front jacket photography: ©Deborah Mazzoleni: *Past Made Perfect*
Back jacket photography (clockwise from top): ©Michael Jensen: *Cabin Fever*;
©Alan Weintraub: *California Comfortable*, ©Kari Haavisto: *Second Thoughts*

Color separations by Radstock Repro
Printed in England by Butler & Tanner Limited

3 5 7 9 10 8 6 4

For bulk purchases and special sales, please contact:
Friedman/Fairfax Publishers
Attention: Sales Department
15 West 26th Street
New York, New York 10010
212/685-6610   FAX 212/685-1307

Visit our website:
http://www.metrobooks.com

Contents

Introduction

Most of us live small; this, despite the plethora of high-volume houses that seem to be sprouting almost overnight across the landscape. When we say "small," we're thinking of 2,000 square feet (180sq.m) or less—which means a lot of family living is compacted into a little space. Those of us who live in such well-defined residences take it as a challenge to make the best use of the houses we have. Making every inch count is what this book is all about.

The real challenge of living fully in smaller quarters is to see that no room is underused. Does your dining room rouse to life two or three times a year when holidays hit and then fall into a museum-like dormancy the rest of the time? Is your living room a space that you simply walk through? Do you have a guest bedroom that spends most of the year with a vacancy sign? If so, rethink and reinvent these spaces to your best advantage. They could probably find new double-duty uses as a home office or media room instead of as repositories for ill-assorted collections of cast-off furniture.

Take a hard, objective look at where you live. In a smaller home, rooms, nooks, crannies, and other architectural elements become very important. They help define areas, create privacy, and allow for creative storage—ways to expand a tiny room or an unused corner. Don't overlook forgotten areas under stairs or in hallways; they provide hidden space for convenient storage or as display areas. And, if you live in a traditional older home, perhaps it's time to make your house fit your lifestyle so that it can be totally lived in. Reconfigure the space you have. Tearing down walls to open up a rabbit warren of rooms is an effective way of letting in light; it has the added benefit of improving the traffic patterns.

When you see a small space that works big, try to pick out the designer's or decorator's tricks that achieve this remarkable effect. Are rooms partially open to one another so that each borrows "visual" space from the other? Or, maybe, a pair of French doors that opens onto a deck lets the eye perceive the outdoor space as part of the indoor room.

Thinking big in a small house helps you to focus on the size and scale of furniture. You may need less to create the effect of more. Here again, enhancing the perception of space is key. A few big statement pieces of furniture arranged perfectly may be exactly what a room needs.

Color plays a crucial role in making a small space seem larger. Remember that lighter tones expand an area, and darker ones reduce space. This is particularly important when trying to unify several small areas. Using a single color throughout a series of rooms can fool the eye into thinking the area is bigger than it really is. This applies not only to walls but to the floor as well. A single expanse of wooden flooring or carpeting, for instance, will unify the different areas, making the adjoining spaces look bigger—another example of the "borrowed-space" technique.

Many of us who live in small homes do not have the luxury of putting on an addition. We can neither expand into the backyard or up into the next floor. Budget considerations or local building codes sometimes place constraints on our ability to enlarge our homes. The real solution lies in being able to see new space in the old. Rearranging rooms, rethinking an area's purposes, and redecorating to fit our needs are the goals of anyone who lives compactly. Doing more with less requires creativity and imagination. It is with great pleasure that we bring you this useful and beautiful book, brimming with ideas to help make your home the "Best Little House™" it can be.

Gale C. Steves,
Editor-in-Chief, HOME® Magazine

Good things come
in small packages. It's a
time-honored expression that can
be beautifully true of houses; diminutive
dwellings, while small in space, can be big
on ideas. And nowhere is the premise manifest
with such clarity as in the shipshape, 1,200-

square-foot (111 sq.m)
retreat that architect
William Witt designed on
Whidbey Island, near
Seattle, as a personal playhouse for his family.

Whidbey Island, which has been designated
a national historic reserve dedicated to the
"preservation of a rural island lifestyle," provided

Bright colors and geometric shapes give this house a playful air. The house's ingenious
floor plan employs a series of levels linked by open stairways.

a picturesque locale for Witt's weekend home. The lagoon-side site had much to recommend it—it's accessible by two ferries as well as by a bridge, and yet, because lots on the lagoon are not considered "prime waterfront" property, the site was eminently affordable. But it also created constraints that necessitated a scaled-down getaway. Although the lot measured 210 feet (64m) deep × 75 feet (22.5m) wide, Witt was restricted to a smaller footprint by three factors: first, a mandated setback from the lagoon; second, the municipally approved location of the septic system in the exact center of his property; and third, the placement of an old, prized indigenous madrona tree. (Witt could double the size of his house, but in so doing would have to uproot the tree,

OPPOSITE: On the main level, the 450-square-foot (42sq.m) kitchen is brightened by salvaged school chairs refurbished with left-over interior paint. ABOVE LEFT: The cheerful painted display case and low table built from leftover pine have distinctive wedge-shaped accents. ABOVE RIGHT: Bill and his daughter, then five, assembled the kitchen's "working wall" of cabinets from IKEA kits.

a decision deferred for the foreseeable future.) Left with a small space in which to build, Witt had to come up with a design with abundant flexibility and creativity.

As a young family involved in creative pursuits (Bill's wife, Wilder, is an educator and illustrator), the Witts wanted a playful house; they did not want to make a "serious statement." They achieved their goal through the interplay of children's-block-like geometric shapes and bright, Crayola-like colors. The house stacks three open, 450-square-foot (42sq.m) "great rooms" linked by open stairways and supported by board-and-batten-sheathed shafts, which contain baths, children's bunks, and a laundry room. The top level looks like a giant latticed gable.

The lowest level, first conceived as an open-sided pavilion for boats, was closed in for the two Witt children because their parents could see "that the kids need their own space—as we do." The vertical shape of the house was influenced by other factors, specifically the proximity of a country inn across the lagoon, as well as other cabins. Luckily, a stand of luxuriant fir trees blocks most views of their neighbors, thus ensuring a feeling of privacy. And elevating the main floor (the eat-in kitchen) guaranteed more views of the water, and fewer of the inn.

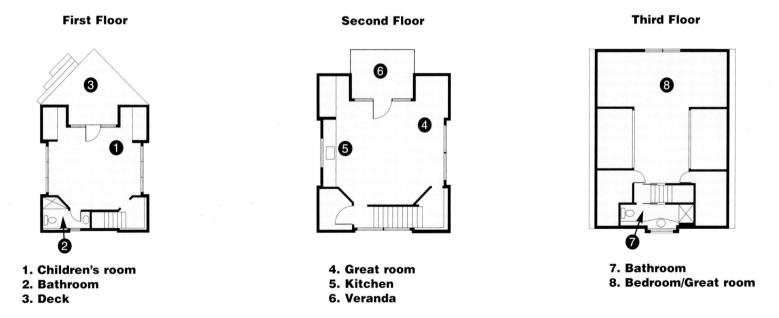

First Floor

Second Floor

Third Floor

1. Children's room
2. Bathroom
3. Deck

4. Great room
5. Kitchen
6. Veranda

7. Bathroom
8. Bedroom/Great room

The children's room opens to a prow-shaped deck shared by the entire family. Bunks were slotted into facing shafts. A hobby counter links one bunk shaft to stair landing shaft; IKEA units stash toys (there are no closets). The fourth shaft houses a bathroom. Floors are spruce.

Thinking big was not what Joanna and Bill Seitz had in mind for their New Mexico home. What they did want was something "small and cozy" that "embodies the area's unique feel of earth, sky, and land." The pueblo-style house, created by architect David Gibbons of Thaddeus Design to occupy twelve acres (4.8ha) of desert just outside Santa Fe, does exactly that. Exterior walls comprise three coats of cement plaster mixed with hay and other natural elements, offering a modern version of the wonderfully textured look of centuries-old adobe.

Home on the Range

An L-shaped porch furnished with a table and plenty of chairs extends the home's living space to encompass the desert landscape. At night, wall lamps cast a golden glow, allowing the family to enjoy the outdoors well into evening.

The house's interior reflects the couple's artistic outlook—he's a photographer, she's the guiding force of a home-furnishings shop, J. Seitz & Co.—and appreciation of the region. The 20 × 24-foot (6 × 7.2m) living and dining room showcases Southwestern-casual pieces, along with antiques and decorative objects that Joanna and Bill have collected. Flooring throughout the home is old brick pressed into sand and coated with a protective sealer. The woodwork is similarly old, recycled from other structures. Interior walls are hand-rubbed mud plaster—dirt mixed with straw and a little water—the colors determined by the mud used. Instead of paint chips, Joanna says, "we looked at samples of mud!"

ABOVE: The large, open main room combines living and dining. The dining area features a country table situated to bask in the light from the windows by day, while an ironwork chandelier supplies nighttime illumination. OPPOSITE: A traditional Southwestern fireplace anchors the living area of the main room. Throughout are pieces collected by Joanna from the Santa Fe region and beyond.

The U-shaped kitchen, with its tile-topped counters, is a wonderful amalgam of vintage and new.

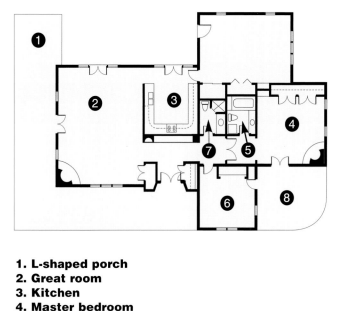

1. **L-shaped porch**
2. **Great room**
3. **Kitchen**
4. **Master bedroom**
5. **Master bathroom**
6. **Bedroom**
7. **Bathroom**
8. **Sunset garden**

Within the house's 2,000 square feet (186sq.m) of usable space is a 12 × 14-foot (3.6 × 4.2m) cutting-edge kitchen made to look at least a century old. "We wanted a vintage kitchen with modern amenities," Joanna says. Up-to-date appliances share the room with older pieces, including a large farm table that provides plenty of work space. A craftsman created the reproduction cabinets that look as authentic as the antiques. Countertops and backsplash are covered in Mexican tiles. Overhead there are salvaged log-like poles, called *vigas*. Joining the vigas together are *latillas*, thin tree limbs that have been split in two, trimmed, and pressed in place. These form the base of a multi-layer roof system that is typical of New Mexico dwellings. "When the roof was being built," Joanna recalls, "our driveway resembled a huge pile of pick-up sticks."

An old farm table serves as a work island in the center, and colorful textiles, ceramics, and collectibles add to the ambiance.

21

The master bedroom, a feast of antique Mexican pieces, is located at the far end of the house, down a corridor drenched in sunshine that pours down from two skylights. French doors expand the 14 × 17-foot (4.2 × 5.2m) space and open to the enclosed sunset garden, which extends to the Seitzes' daughter's bedroom. "There are no patios in the Southwest," Joanna says. "There are walled gardens instead. We sit out here to see the sun drop down over the Jemez Mountains. But our main family living area is the *portal*." This L-shaped covered porch, which goes along the east and north sides of the house, is the place where both daytime and nighttime scenery is appreciated. It's furnished so that the family can share meals or snacks there, or just relax and read. An expansion, still being planned, will let the Seitzes enjoy their home on the range full-time someday.

ABOVE LEFT: The master bath has white fixtures and Mexican tiles, the latter in a restful cream color.
ABOVE RIGHT AND OPPOSITE: A fanciful, one-of-a-kind bed by Tommy Simpson dominates the master bedroom, while antique Mexican pieces and a traditionally shaped fireplace complete the rustic Southwestern feel.

For this Chicago-area family of six, each of whom loves to ski, hike, and fish, the ideal getaway was a log cabin in the modern-day wilderness of Wyoming, within sight of the dramatic Teton Mountains. Wanting a place that would be "small and manageable," the couple turned to Alpine Log Homes to design and handcraft a

vacation house on ranch land they had purchased near Jackson Hole. Working with Alpine's architectural staff, they ended up with a comfortable 1,000-square-foot (93sq.m) house that is totally at home within the area's majestic landscape.

Reassembled, log by log, at the site, the finished house was sealed with a type of latex chinking that expands and contracts as the weather changes. The chinking was left white for a striated look that enriches both the façade and interior walls. In another nod to Mother Nature the house was built with a "cold roof" system. Essentially a sandwich of two roofs—one built on top of the other, with a few inches of air space in between—the cold roof system allows snow to stand until spring thaw.

The house's interior is laid out in a simple T-shape: two bedrooms and two baths form the crossbar, with a loft/storage area above. Occupying the stem is the "great room," which is a combined family room-kitchen-dining area. "We've always liked the charm and Western feeling of log homes," say the homeowners. In keeping with that relaxed Western sensibility, the interior design was kept simple. The room gets its rustic yet cozy personality from accessories that feature cowboy-and-Indian motifs, buffalo-plaid fabrics, and other Wild West–themed pieces. One particularly stunning Western element can be found in the great room: the massive stone fireplace, made of river rock, its screen forged by Wyoming artisans.

The impressive fireplace that dominates the great room is made of river rock. Comfortable, casual furniture makes the room cozy and inviting. The buffalo-plaid slipcovers and pillows, made from tablecloths, suit the room's homey charm, and cowboy-themed placemats and napkins add a touch of Western whimsy.

First Floor

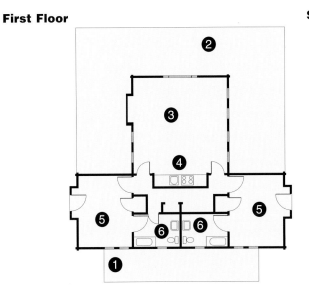

Second Floor

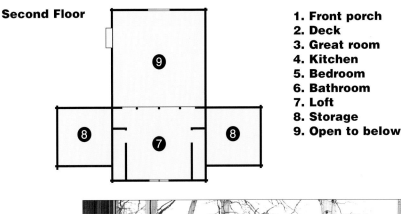

1. Front porch
2. Deck
3. Great room
4. Kitchen
5. Bedroom
6. Bathroom
7. Loft
8. Storage
9. Open to below

The starting point in designing the house was to consider its site, which is spectacular. The designers oriented the house toward a meadow and a creek, so that the generously sized windows could take full advantage of the wonderful vistas offered, including, looming in the distance beyond the woods, snow-capped Grand Teton Mountain.

After the design plans were finalized, the logs were pre-cut from lodge pole pine (only standing dead timber was used, no living trees were sacrificed), and the notches hand-fit. The house was then preassembled. Once approved, the structure was dismantled, and each log numbered before being shipped to the site. At that point the contractor took over the project. It was the contractor's job to grade the raw site, bring in the utilities, sink a foundation, and rebuild the house.

A huge bay window overlooking a meadow lends a feeling of spaciousness to the compact dining area in the great room. The window was left uncurtained, making the view an integral part of the decor.

The owners chose wide-plank oak floorings, which adds to a feeling of openness in the 21 × 25-foot (6.4 × 7.6m) great room and also unites individual areas within it. Knotty, rough-hewn wood, wire-brushed so the grain pokes through, created a

rougher, more rustic look. Built-ins, including the kitchen work island and bench, were crafted to the owners' specifications, and provide hidden storage space. All interior and exterior doors were handmade of cedar planks.

Despite the house's compact nature, the owners say they never get in each other's way. That may be thanks in part to a 12-foot (3.6m)-wide deck that surrounds three sides of the house and more than doubles its usable living space. Additionally, a cathedral ceiling inside rises more than 16 feet (4.8m) above the great room, which makes the house feel larger. Finally, the built-ins provide bonus storage space for controlling clutter.

"And the logs add so much character that we didn't need to do a lot of decorating. What we wanted was a low-upkeep cabin we could just lock up and leave. There is no fuss."

ABOVE: A loft over the kitchen can do double duty as storage or an extra sleeping area. Tiles top the eating/work surfaces.
OPPOSITE: Custom beds and window seats enhance the 12 × 15-foot (3.6 × 4.5m) bedrooms. The Western motif extends even to the bed linens and seat covers. Concealed below the cozy window seats are large storage spaces.

This compact dwelling, designed by architect Mark Griesbach for himself and his wife, Kate Konrad, sits snug in a pine forest near Tallahassee, Florida. Taking inspiration from the barns of Florida's tobacco country, Griesbach combined a steeply pitched roof, clapboard siding, and high window openings into a

striking 1,350-square-foot (125sq.m) design. In spite of its clean-lined crispness, the house looks as if it has always been standing there in the woods, an impression that the ecologically minded architect intended. "Not one tree was felled to make room for this place," he says proudly.

The proportions of this home are modeled on those of traditional Florida barns. At the rear, a deck stretches out into the pine forest, attractively expanding usable living space for most of the year. INSET: At the front, a bright yellow door extends a warm welcome.

Following in the footsteps of Thoreau, Griesbach and Konrad went to the woods and built a house. Preserving a view of their own pond came first in Griesbach's design for the site. The couple also embraced Thoreau's advice to "simplify, simplify, simplify," which is one reason the interior of their small house looks so airy and spacious. Thanks to simplicity of line and spareness of furniture, the main floor seems much larger than its 900 square feet (84sq.m). This illusion is enhanced by the two-story living room ceiling, which soars 18 feet (5.4m) high. On the second level is a loft space; its openwork railing, fitted with glass for safety, allows the spatial flow to continue. Sunlight pouring in through upper-level windows and expanses of glass on front and rear elevations enhance the feeling of space, an effect that is magnified by white walls and glass-block partitions.

One of the factors that inspired this particular diminutive design was Griesbach's belief that he could "build something without spending an arm and a leg." By keeping

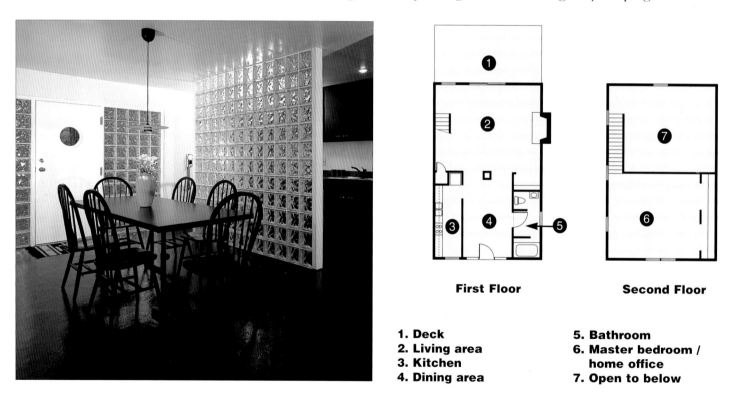

First Floor   **Second Floor**

1. Deck   5. Bathroom
2. Living area   6. Master bedroom /
3. Kitchen   home office
4. Dining area   7. Open to below

The open, expansive quality of the house owes much to the architect's use of glass block. Panels of it flank the front door, funneling dappled sun into the interior. Another panel allows light to spill into the potentially dark galley-style kitchen, softening the separation between it and the dining room.

the dimensions modest, using cost-efficient materials, and acting as his own general contractor, he kept costs down without compromising architectural integrity.

Its small size notwithstanding, this is a house that lives big enough to accommodate the owners, occasional weekend guests, and a child or two should the couple decide to start a family. The second level, which currently combines the master bedroom with a home office, could be easily divided into two bedrooms, and plumbing for a small bath has already been roughed in.

Griesbach knew he had reached his goal when his wife paid him the ultimate compliment. "I love living in this house," she said.

A bold, boxed-in staircase (upper right) leads to the loft bedroom. The railing across the loft uses a variation on the Greek-cross theme, says Griesbach. Another classical touch is the column that bisects the opening into the dining space. "The Greek Revival column provides a visual separation between living and dining rooms," says the architect, "and it's also my reference to the architecture of the Deep South."

Built with an eye
on the future and low
maintenance in mind, this very
adaptable house serves as a vacation
getaway now and can become a retirement
home later. The Joneses, married professionals,
wanted flexibility and energy efficiency for their
new weekend home located in Bucks
County, Pennsylvania—and they
found just the house they wanted in

Keeping up with the Joneses

this HOME® Magazine mail-order plan, which they
modified to meet their personal needs. Working
with the original architect, Larry James, they
built a cabin-style 1,233-square-foot (114sq.m)
house with classic post-and-beam construction.

With an open front porch and a screened-in back porch, this house offers plenty of opportunity for outdoor living.
INSET: At nightfall the house glows as invitingly as a campfire in the woods.

Set on a gentle slope that creates a mostly above-ground basement for future expansion, the dwelling has stylish gray roofing tiles, an open front porch set over crawl space, and a screened-in back porch. To make the house look as if it had always been part of the 13-acre (5.2ha) site, the Joneses asked their landscaper to determine which trees to save and which to sacrifice during construction. He designed the planting areas around the house and had the fence built from cedar trees cut on the property. The house's shutters were designed by James from a picture the Joneses sent him, and assembled by the builder.

Intending for the house to "grow" along with them, converting eventually from weekend retreat to accessible primary residence, the Joneses kept to one guiding principle for the interior—furnishings had to be economically efficient, low-maintenance, and versatile. In the 24-foot (7.3m)-long family living space, for instance, which soars to a two-story height under a cathedral ceiling, a cluster of eight windows fills the room with daylight yet is positioned high enough to allow maximum wall space. As a result, there's plenty of room available to house handsome cherry bookcases and a propane gas fireplace. The range, on-demand water heater, furnace, and low-energy-usage space heater are also fed by propane, which burns at a high rate of efficiency, saving energy and money over years of use. A ceiling fan helps keep the room comfortable.

The Joneses chose a number of innovative and energy-saving products to make their house more comfortable and convenient for now and in the years to come. They opted for fiberglass insulation, which retains heat in the winter and repels it in summer. It also creates a vapor barrier that cuts condensation and mildew damage in damp areas. The state-of-the-art gas furnace promises up to 93.5-percent heat efficiency, uses less electricity than one powered by a standard motor, and, with balanced air flow, provides flexibility and comfort. Even the back porch is efficient, open to the air but insect-free, thanks to easily-installed screens. For roofing, the Joneses used durable, economical fiberglass shingles. But economy was not the only consideration; design was important, too. The wood blinds at the windows are a stylish, contemporary interpretation of the traditional venetian blinds. A simple twist of the control wand makes it easy to adjust

The combined living/dining room features a fireplace to warm the conversation area at one end, with dining table at the other end. The room is unified by the honey-toned oak plank flooring, the soaring ceiling, and a bank of windows through which light pours into the room.

heat containment and light, as well as the view. Nothing was sacrificed to achieve the goals of convenience and enlightened efficiency.

The flow-together living/dining room has comfy, durable, upholstered furniture for flexible seating. A "display" cocktail table and storage end table are practical additions to the room. And both ends of the room have porch access: the living area opens onto the front porch, the dining area onto the screened-in rear porch.

In the dining area, a pine table and chairs offer an alternate work space as well as an eating surface. Cherry bookcases along the wall provide convenient storage and display.

The master bedroom, tucked right under the loft, is furnished with Shaker-like simplicity. Interior designer Charles Riley chose each piece carefully so as not to crowd the 12½ × 16-foot (3.8 x 4.8m) space, and still leave enough room for a queen-size pencil post bed. There is plenty of light—from windows looking out on the side yard and back porch—and there is privacy. The loft stairs, which lead to a separate seating area, distinguish this room from the family living space. The double closets back up to one wall of the kitchen, creating two good sound buffers, helping to reinforce the room's sense of peace and restfulness.

ABOVE LEFT: Mixing simple Shaker-style pieces of natural wood and black-painted wood pieces lends elegance to the master bedroom. The door leads to the master bath. ABOVE RIGHT: The lingerie chest has a "secret" compartment for hanging jewelry.

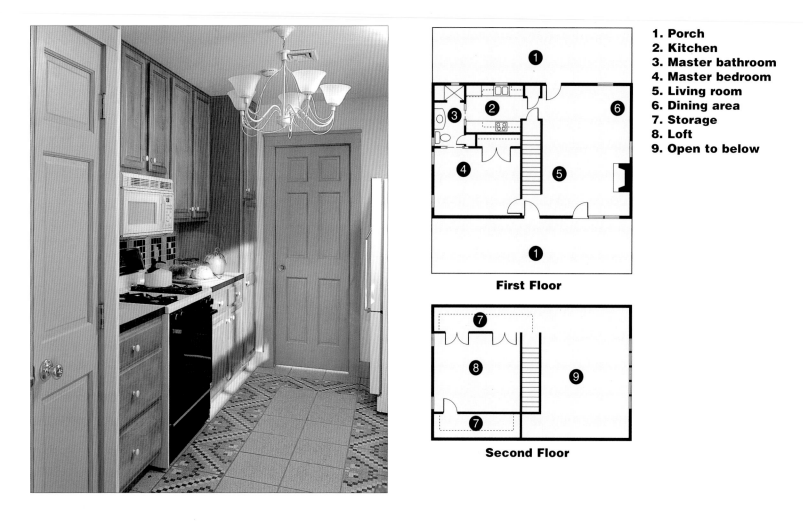

1. Porch
2. Kitchen
3. Master bathroom
4. Master bedroom
5. Living room
6. Dining area
7. Storage
8. Loft
9. Open to below

First Floor

Second Floor

The 9 × 17-foot (2.7 x 5.1m) galley kitchen, with its light maple cabinetry, is packed with appliances as well as smaller but nonetheless welcome amenities to ease the chores of food preparation and cooking. Cupboards and storage drawers are placed so that whatever utensil, vessel, or serving piece is needed is within easy reach. Flush against the easy-care countertop are black-and-white tiles that coordinate with the low-maintenance tile flooring, the design of which calls to mind an Amish quilt pattern.

The dramatic contrast of black and white has been used to great effect in the kitchen. The design of the tile backsplash behind the countertop complements the mosaic pattern of the floor tiles.

The plan of the kitchen, like the house itself, is simple but smart. Food prep and cooking occur on one side of the room, cleanup and put-away on the other. The open end of the kitchen flows out of the dining area. It is separate from the public space on the first floor but not totally removed from whatever's going on in the rest of the house. At the far end of the kitchen a pocket door provides another access to the bath, which, right now, is the house's single all-purpose facility. It is both a guest bath and a master bath, and because of its size, there is room for only a combination tub and shower. A capacious vanity holds the sink and enough cupboards and drawers to satisfy all of the couple's bath and grooming needs. And for safety's sake, a grab bar on the wall next to the tub ensures easy entry for bathers of all ages.

The tiling in the bathroom echoes the distinctive quilt-inspired tile treatment in the kitchen.
A smaller, diagonal interpretation has been used on the shower wall, creating a unified theme in the room.

The guest room in the loft is open to the family living space below and to the windows that bring light into the house. The room itself contains only 230 square feet (21sq.m), but its overall area includes two storage spaces that add 151 square feet (14sq.m) of utility to the room. Behind a single door on one wall and a pair of doors on the opposite wall are fully heated, easily accessible storage areas. Eight feet (2.4m) high at the door, they slope to three or four feet (about a meter) to tuck in under the eaves.

In a small house, these hidden utility spaces are a godsend, underscoring the fact that small doesn't have to mean cramped—and good design doesn't waste an inch.

ABOVE: The sleep sofa is a dual-purpose piece that makes the loft space work as a room for guests to sleep in as well as a den that invites relaxation. Sunlight floods the space from windows on two sides, which offer views of the woods outside. OPPOSITE: A wing chair and an upholstered rocker make the guest room a comfortable getaway spot for reading or conversing. Available when needed are a big-screen TV, VCR, and stereo system installed in cabinets, making the room a home entertainment center as well.

Having an architect in the family can be very handy. When Bob and Fay Farris decided to move to Tannin Village, Alabama, a growing community on the Gulf Coast designed to re-create the experience of old-time small-town living, they wanted a new house that would both fit into the planned design scheme of the town and accommodate their need for an easy-access retirement dwelling. Their son, Chicago, Illinois–based architect Roger Farris, came up with just what they wanted. His design for this three-story seaside residence is an elegant example of time-honored Southern design that has been scaled down with no sacrifice of its architectural stateliness.

Drawing on traditional Southern style, the house is at once stately and simple. Its columned front porch offers a pleasant outdoor "room" for enjoying the sea breezes.

The columns, covered porches, and tall windows bring to mind the gracious homes of the American South, where both of the Farrises spent their childhoods. Exterior living areas—in the form of sun-splashed roof decks and shady covered porches—also contributed to the look of the house. "We wanted to create pleasant spaces for sitting outside in nice weather," says the architect, "and we also wanted to make the rooms feel larger by opening them up to adjacent porches." In all, the Farrises agree, they got a house that "lives much larger than it really is."

Although it measures only 872 square feet (81sq.m), the first floor is so skillfully laid out that the owners never feel cramped. "This is an easy-living house," says Bob Farris. And from certain angles, he points out, it actually looks like a larger house. One larger-than-life space is the living room, where French doors open to porches at either end, extending sightlines and visually increasing the space. Another such area is the second floor, where rooms, doors, and windows are arranged so that the eye travels from the front of the house straight through to the back. The second floor also offers outdoor living areas—a sunny deck built on top of each covered porch, accessible from both the guest bedroom and the guest bath.

Roger Farris employed several other techniques to make the small house "live big"— a strategic use of glass, for instance. In the living room, three sets of French doors on front and back walls, tall windows flanking the fireplace, and a series of smaller windows

ABOVE: Located a block from the Gulf of Mexico, in Tannin, Alabama, this house wears a sunny palette of sherbet colors—peach with green trim at the windows. OPPOSITE: Comfortable and welcoming, the living room is filled with sunlight and bright colors. Adding a dash of pattern, slipcovers on the sofa coordinate with solid and striped decorative pillows.

near the ceiling flood the room with light, making it appear to be much bigger than its actual dimensions. Unlike their previous home, where the large living room was seldom used—"only a few times a year," Farris recalls—this living area invites company. The light-filled space is further accented with a welcoming color scheme of tropical colors.

The architect also manipulated proportions to give the house its sense of grandeur and size. The living room ceiling rises to 14½ feet (4.4m) high, and the windows he

The living room is flanked on either side by porches, which can be easily accessed by two sets of French doors, one on each side of the room. Light from the doors and the windows above them floods the room with light.

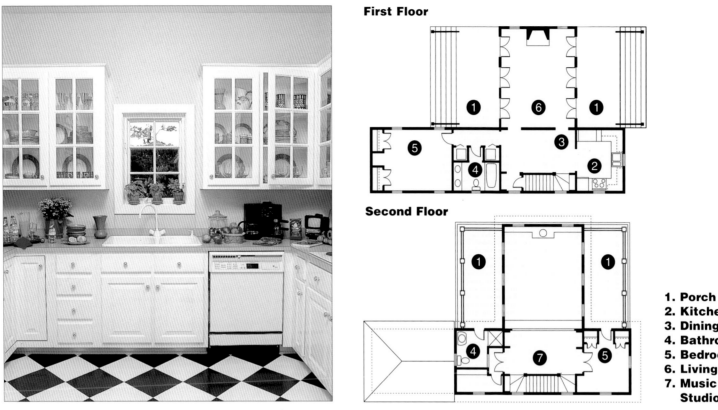

First Floor

Second Floor

1. Porch
2. Kitchen
3. Dining room
4. Bathroom
5. Bedroom
6. Living room
7. Music room/
   Studio

chose are taller and narrower than standard sizes. The French doors are also unconventionally proportioned. "They're only four feet [1.2m] wide," says Farris, "which is smaller than those typically found in new homes." The result, he claims, is that "you think you're looking at something much bigger."

The three-story floor plan was developed with one guiding principle: "not to waste any space." Every square foot of living area is utilized, every room gets plenty of use, and there are practically no hallways. You move from one room directly into another, a space-planning technique that makes the small house seem much larger than it really is.

To simplify housekeeping and eliminate stair-climbing for the senior Farrises as they grow older, Farris placed the spaces they use most often—living and dining rooms, kitchen and master suite—on the 872-square-foot (81sq.m) first floor. On the second

The principle underlying the design of the compact yet very functional kitchen was that everything should be "easy to get to." The simple black-and-white color scheme resulted in a crisp, fresh-looking room that belies its small size.

floor, which contains only 397 square feet (37sq.m), are a guest bedroom and bath, and a music room that doubles as a sitting room for guests. Dominating this space is a grand piano that Roger Farris, an accomplished musician, plays when he visits. The top floor of the house is a light-filled aerie reserved as a combination art studio for Roger, who paints still lifes and portraits, and a spot for scenic appreciation of the Gulf of Mexico vistas.

Although the exterior colors of the house capture the more sedate shades typical of seaside living, the interior of the house is the exception to the rule of using white to expand small spaces. Lively patterns in easy-care cotton and a vibrant range of hues throughout the living areas add personality and style to the design scheme.

To create a cheerful guest room, Farris chose what he calls "Naples Yellow," complemented by aqua and tangerine pillows and plaid sheets. The room opens onto a sunny deck.

Spectacular views plus an abundance of natural light make the top-floor studio ideal for painting. Built-in shelves line the walls beneath the windows, adding ample storage for art supplies and books, with the ledges serving to display the artist's work.

This "Best Little House"

isn't brand new, but seventy

years old, a thoughtfully renovated

Arts-and-Crafts-style cottage. The owners made

the most of what they had—three bedrooms and

two baths in 1,450 square feet (135sq.m)—to

create a comfortable home for a family of three.

Although it was built in the

1920s in the Carrollton district of

New Orleans, the house, says the owner, architect

Edward H. Wikoff, "is not your typical New

Orleans kind of house. It lacks the 12-foot (3.6m)

ceilings and all the gingerbread of the original

'shotgun' houses in the Garden District." But the

house, when Wikoff and his wife, designer Nora

Westayer, bought it, was of "good stock," allowing

The wood trim on this Arts and Crafts-style cottage is cypress, a New Orleans tradition to counter the ever-present termite menace.

Comfortable seating and timeless design lend an appealing coziness to the cottage's living room.

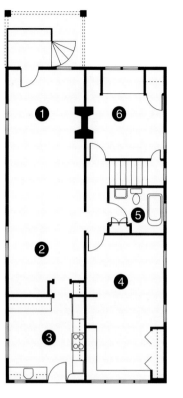

1. Living area
2. Dining area
3. Kitchen
4. Master bedroom
5. Bathroom
6. Bedroom

them to keep much of the original house intact and just do some "sprucing up." With a sensible layout plus a shed-roof addition dating from the '60s, the Wikoffs' cottage proved an ideal residence for a small family: the upstairs bedroom and bath comprise a separate suite for their daughter.

Other than repainting, the only change made to the front exterior was a new door. "It's actually an old door that was salvaged," says the architect. "More in keeping with houses of this vintage."

The main living space, a 12 × 32-foot (3.6 × 9.7m) combination living-dining room with diamond-shaped custom vinyl flooring, contains an eclectic mix of furniture, the most special being an armoire found in the homeowner's great-grandmother's basement. In order to make room for the piece, a doorway to the kitchen was moved so that a niche could be built. The timeless design of the living room furniture, including a cabinet that keeps the television hidden from view, complements the antique armoire.

In the living room, a cabinet with Arts and Crafts styling displays collectibles and houses the TV.

Moving the kitchen doorway didn't change the square room's 12 × 12-foot (3.6 × 3.6m) measurements, but it did create a straight path from the front of the house to the back, so that, says Wikoff, "either of us working in the kitchen can keep an eye on our daughter." It also added a long wall with enough space to accommodate a built-in desk/work surface. Another bonus: at long last there would be room for a breakfast table, a large glass-top style that manages to fit the space perfectly. The doorway transom, added to align with the heightened armoire niche in the living room, holds some of the vintage art pottery—Roseville pieces—the Wikoffs collect; other examples—Hall china and Fiestaware—are displayed in wall-mounted shelving over the desk. Standard cabinetry was customized with a moss-green accent color and seeded glass, an antique-

ABOVE LEFT: The kitchen underwent the most significant reorganization, with the doorway shifted and the window, originally located in the kitchen corner, moved to be centered over the sink. Glass doors and painted trim transformed standard cabinetry into something special. ABOVE RIGHT: Display over the desk in the kitchen offers a home for collectibles. The vinyl flooring, used in both the kitchen and the living room, was custom-cut into different shapes for each room. The effect is one of distinct individual rooms within a unified whole.

looking bubble glass that, says the architect, "creates a nice effect." Wood trim topping the doorway and edging the solid-surface countertops was crafted to echo the crown molding at the top of the cabinets. The extra-tall backsplash is glazed tile in a running-bond pattern that recalls early twentieth-century design.

A wall of windows overlooking the backyard makes the 12 × 20-foot (3.6 × 6m) master bedroom sun-bright and spacious in feeling. "This is the best room in the house," says the homeowner. As elsewhere, the Wikoffs used or adapted much of what previous owners had already created to make the most of the living areas. In the master bedroom, a closet, overhead storage, and a wall of built-in cabinetry situated below the casement windows offer plentiful storage. The bedroom flooring, original to the house, is heart pine. A barely visible wooden threshold divides the sleeping area from what had once been a porch. Walls here are off-white; in the sleeping area the Wikoffs rag-rolled the walls in moss-green and applied glaze for a textured effect. The area comfortably accommodates a king-size bed, dressed in pillows and duvet cover in coordinating shades of green. Windows flanking the bed are covered with salvaged shutters that once graced the exterior of a stately old New Orleans home. Cut to fit and then refinished, they help control light and provide privacy from nearby neighbors.

In the bedroom, built-in cabinetry was spruced up and given new chrome hardware.
The chaise longue and small table are set up for reading or daydreaming.

Without adding a
square foot, Robert Young,
a Los Angeles designer-builder,
transformed this dated, diminutive
cottage into a model home for modern living. His strategy? Combine the interior's many small rooms into large ones, keep design details consistent, and build on outdoor areas that extend space.

Before renovation, this 1920s California cottage was typical of  its genre, loaded with architectural charm but woefully inefficient for today's busy lifestyles. "It was probably a kit house ordered from a catalog," says Young, who masterminded the house's makeover for homeowner Matthew Knight.

The arched entryway, original to the house, has true cottage charm.

ABOVE: A small house needs to put all its space to work. In the foyer, a painted desk sits against the wall. The warm tones of the hardwood floor are accented by a multihued rug. RIGHT: Comfy upholstered pieces arranged around the fireplace create coziness in the living room. Echoing the symmetry of the windows, sconces flank the mantelpiece, adding soft light and old-fashioned charm.

"Inside were a lot of tiny cut-up rooms; that's how they did small houses back then." One of the things that attracted Knight to this, his first house, was the practical aspect—affordability was essential. Another reason was more aesthetic—he liked the old-fashioned look. "It was kind of a handyman's special, very affordable because the interior was a mess," says Young, "but fortunately the structure was sound." Young remained conscious of cost as he planned his redesign. He brought the cottage up to date without adding space, turning it into a true "best little house."

An effective way to make a small house look and feel bigger, says Young, is to create a sense of spatial flow by repeating design elements throughout. In Matthew Knight's cottage, he established this with several elements. The same soft gray-green "aged-looking" paint color appears on all the walls; the hardwood floors are found everywhere except the bathrooms; and the extra-deep 1920s-style moldings are consistent from room to room. The result of this attention to detail is a little house that lives big.

Although Young did not expand the 1,500-square-foot (139sq.m) house, he did rearrange the space. In the bedroom wing, for example, he carved up the existing hall and single bathroom to create separate suites, each with its own entrance and bath. Another space-enhancer—a new deck that extends living areas year-round.

During the makeover process, Young had to wrestle with privacy issues as well as spatial ones. Longer than it is wide, the house was fitted with side-elevation windows that let in light but also faced neighbors only 12 feet (3.6m) away. "To get privacy you'd have to cover all the windows and lose the light," says Young. His solution was to replace

A mix of old and new gives the living room a sense of history without compromising on comfort. The bench, with its woven leather seat and back, only looks old; it is actually a new piece.

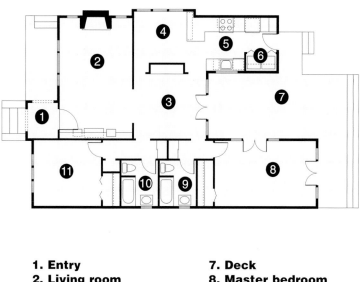

1. Entry
2. Living room
3. Dining room
4. Family room
5. Kitchen
6. Laundry
7. Deck
8. Master bedroom
9. Master bath
10. Bath
11. Bedroom

most of these side windows with leaded glass clerestories that, he says, let in as much light as the originals did, without compromising privacy. In the master bedroom, which faces the rear, he installed a whole wall of glass.

In the living room, privacy was not such an issue. This meant the designer could leave in place the two side-elevation windows that flank the focal point of the room, the fireplace. Here, the dark-green tile surround and granite hearth are new additions, but Young saved the original handsome wood mantel. The windows give the room a classic architectural symmetry.

Opening from the living room is the dining room. Typically, in small houses built during the 1920s, the dining room is a separate—and usually undersized—space; but in this cottage, the L-shaped configuration of the room creates a generous flow of space. Maximizing that feeling of space are French doors that lead out to a deck.

The family room, once a tiny breakfast area, is now open to the kitchen, making both spaces feel larger. The granite kitchen counter marks the spot where the wall once stood. The black-cherry cabinet holds a TV.

Much more typical of the interior architecture of the period is the dining room's built-in china cabinet, which Young spruced up and highlighted with white paint. Kitchen cabinets were designed to echo the cabinet's vintage styling. The arch above the cabinet is one of the recurring design features in the house that Young decided to maintain

Situated in an arch, the newly painted china cabinet shows off collectibles, while the classic styling of the new cherry dining table and chairs makes for elegant seating.

and emphasize in the new and improved design scheme he created. "If a house has good character," he says, "you should let it guide you. We updated this cottage to accommodate modern living, but because we let its spirit direct us, we also retained many of the period details."

Adding new furniture and Oriental rugs to some of the owner's original pieces, New York City designer Charles Riley gave the interiors a comfortable look in keeping with the house's casual charm.

ABOVE LEFT: The brand new master bath sports a pedestal sink and black-and-white tiles that work with the 1920s architecture. Young designed the medicine cabinet and arched tub opening. ABOVE RIGHT: In the master bedroom, a pencil-post bed provides a dramatic focus. French doors lining one wall open to a new rear deck. Wood blinds add period flavor.

This sad, long-neglected bungalow in Sarasota, Florida, more than five decades old, was a textbook case of a buyer-beware fixer-upper. Yet, where everyone else saw an eyesore, schoolteacher Norma Ballard recognized great potential.

A Lesson in Renovation

Ballard hadn't intended to move from her Sarasota gulfside condo when she tagged along on her sister-in-law's house hunt one April day. But just a single look at the little rundown house situated in Sarasota's up-and-coming West-of-the-Trail neighborhood changed her mind. "I was somehow drawn to it," Ballard recalls. "Even though it was a

The house originally suffered from shabby covered patios, front and rear. With a little remodeling and decorating magic, they became screened rooms in keeping with the Florida lifestyle, complete with weatherproof wicker furniture.

mess, it had a certain charm, and I'd wanted to remodel a house since I was a little kid."

Built in 1943, the house had been sitting empty for a year when Ballard saw it, and it looked terrible. The yard was overgrown, and inside the house, floorboards were rotting and the fireplace had fallen. In addition, the rooms were small and dark. Ballard, however, focused only on the house's virtues—she saw a house with charming nooks and crannies and envisioned a "wonderful backyard" with a pool. "In my heart," she says with the optimism of the dedicated elementary school teacher she is, "I saw it shiny and new." By the end of the summer, the house was all hers.

By tearing down a wall between the living room and the former dining room, Ballard was able to open up the living space dramatically. A reading alcove opens off the living room; the former dining room became a family room.

Working with an architect and a contractor, Ballard began remodeling, starting by screening in patios and replacing windows. Next, she knocked down walls to open up the interior space and make a large combined living/family room. But, she admits, "I went into it with more excitement than knowledge." By February, the project had bogged down. Then Ballard visited interior designer Ed Biggs and his partner, Naomi Oliver. "She told me there were just too many decisions," Biggs recalls. "I told her that's part of what I could do for her."

ABOVE LEFT: In the living room, the fireplace was given a much-needed face-lift with a new brick surround and enlarged mantel that displays prized collectibles. Situated around the hearth, chairs and an ottoman create a conversation area.
ABOVE RIGHT: Ballard created a closed-in patio that opens off the living room. Lattice panels add privacy without blocking light and breezes, making this little spot a delightful place to read or enjoy a moment of solitude.

To unify the interiors, the designers helped her choose oak flooring, as well as a pale yellow paint she liked so much that it became the exterior color, too. Against this calming background, they assembled an eclectic collection of brightly colored furnishings and accessories that harmonized with Ballard's own possessions, including antiques and framed art by her students.

The new dining room is a cozy space that features an antique sideboard and casual, comfortable plaid chairs. When open, the French doors rest flush against the wall, giving full access from the dining room to the backyard patio.

Originally planned as a library, the new dining room includes a recess that was intended for bookshelves but perfectly fits the homeowner's antique sideboard. French doors fold outward and flush against the wall, completely opening the room to the rear patio for larger parties. Comfortable plaid wicker chairs complement the intimate circular dining table and reflect the easy informality of Florida living.

The kitchen, Ballard recalls, needed lots of work. "It had a domed ceiling with plastic light panels that had all turned yellow; a brick floor you knew you'd never be able to keep clean; and old, dark wood cabinets." Without changing the dimensions or configuration of the layout, designer Biggs visually enlarged the room by eliminating the overhead lighting panels, thus effectively raising the ceiling. All-white cabinets, appliances,

ABOVE LEFT: The kitchen's white-on-white color scheme makes for a clean, spacious feeling. Handpainted ceramic-tile backsplashes provide color and set off the cabinets. Brightly colored plates sit above the casement windows. ABOVE RIGHT: The copper hood was an original element of the house that was deemed worth saving. Set off against the brick wall, it connects the house to its past.

walls, tile, and trim—combined with the oak floor—create a spacious feeling. The plastic light panels have been replaced; a new overhead fixture plus over- and under-cabinet lighting make the kitchen bright and allow light to be focused where it is needed. Splashes of color come from ceramic tiles that were hand-painted by local artists, and a collection of brightly colored plates. Lending distinctive style to the cooking space is a massive copper hood, original to the kitchen, and offset by a brick wall. "I couldn't have designed the room better if I had tried," says Ballard.

With its high, vaulted ceiling, step-up reading area, and "memory" ledge to display antique toys, the master bedroom is Ballard's favorite place. Along with a fresh coat of

ABOVE LEFT: Among the home's "nooks" is a step-up sitting area in the master bedroom. The addition of a comfy wing chair, paintings by Ballard's students, and a collection of old toys transformed an odd space into a splendid spot to sit and relax.
ABOVE RIGHT: The master bath neatly accommodates a whirlpool tub, separate shower, and vanity.

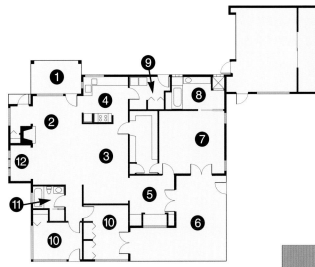

1. **Front patio**
2. **Living room**
3. **Family room**
4. **Kitchen**
5. **Dining room**
6. **Rear patio**
7. **Master bedroom**
8. **Master bath**
9. **Laundry room**
10. **Bedroom**
11. **Bath**
12. **Reading alcove**

paint and some Berber carpeting, designer Biggs added a wealth of touches that bring the cozy room to life. Chief among them are antique-inspired furniture and the lively aquamarine bedspread and draperies (this color also appears in the master bath). A touch of whimsy comes from a bright yellow wicker chair and a tall birdhouse on the ledge. Such attention to detail, sums up Ballard, "is what finally made this house work." Adds Biggs: "One of the hardest things to do is take your possessions from one home to a new space, especially when it's from a contemporary condo to a 1940s bungalow, but everything was important to her, so we made it all work."

Across from the seating nook, the bed features an antique-inspired headboard. A colorful fabric for the bedspread and draperies adds zest, while the antique toys attest to Ballard's passion for collection.

"If at first you don't succeed, try, try again," could be this home- owner's motto. Dan Maddux originally bought a four-acre (1.6ha) property, part of an upstate New York dairy farm dotted with apple and pear trees, because he fell in love with the old barn. "The stalls still had the cows' names

on them," he reminisces. An execu- tive for a nonprofit organization who spends half his time traveling, Maddux was eager to create a weekend haven where he could relax and pursue his avocation as a painter. But his dream of converting the slate- roofed structure into a residence was shattered when local banks did not share his vision.

The house kit was customized to the site selected by Maddux, who hired a local builder to erect the shell and complete the home.

height defines various areas. The cozy hearth end of the living room has a standard-height beamed ceiling. At the room's other end, the ceiling rises, barn-style, to the rafters of the roof, which is pierced with skylights. In the dining area, the ceiling drops down again for greater intimacy.

Before filling the rooms with Gustav Stickley reproduction furniture and Arts and Crafts pottery and other collectibles, Maddux "aged" the walls himself, using two coats of Benjamin Moore's Golden Amber Grain that he topped with a layer of Minwax's Satin Honey Pine stain. "People say that it makes the house look really old," Maddux notes with satisfaction.

ABOVE LEFT: A window seat in the dining room is made cozy with pillows embroidered by Maddux's Grandma Esther. ABOVE RIGHT: Attention to detail is the hallmark of this home's style, as seen in this evocative arrangement of Arts and Crafts pieces, including a painting by Anita Munman above a sideboard that shows off some of Maddux's pottery collection. OPPOSITE: Another Munman painting sets the stage for a collection of Roycroft, Weller, Roseville, and Stickley Craftsman pottery.

ABOVE: The Stickley dining room furniture glows in the light of the room's antique chandelier, which is fitted with new mica shades. OPPOSITE: The kitchen and dining areas are divided by a tile-topped peninsula that doubles as a spot for a quick bite. Cherry cabinetry and coppery tiles evoke the Arts and Crafts era, while modern appliances ensure ease of food preparation.

"Rather than use a decorator, I like to do things myself," says Maddux, who was determined to give the two floors of 1,268 square feet (118sq.m) of living space in his new house a mellowed "antique" look. While planning the decor, he saw an article in HOME® about a new Craftsman-style house displaying Anita Munman's paintings, and became an instant convert to the nineteenth-century Arts and Crafts style, which emphasizes fine handiwork and simple decoration. For the color scheme, he chose favorite colors—eggplant, olive green, yellow, and orange, with touches of copper, a favorite metal.

In the dining room, Maddux combined Stickley pieces, including a graceful centennial cellarette and needlepoint rug, with "the right tone of eggplant to set everything off." He asked the Habitat design team to add a bay window to the plan, then cozied it up with a window seat piled high with handmade Arts and Crafts-style pillows.

The kitchen shows off how well the simplicity of a barn structure fits into the Arts and Crafts aesthetic. The result is a successful merger of clean lines and artistic accents.

Made of solid South American cherry, the Shaker-style cabinets match the fir

and pine in the rest of the house. Attention to detail abounds, from patinated brass hardware to copper-luster tiles that line the walls, adorned with intricate mosaics. Shiny white tiles top the counters. Over the stainless-steel range, a collage of relief tiles depicts a bumble bee, an owl, and other natural subjects. Flanked by two plate racks, it stylishly hides the exhaust pipe.

ABOVE and OPPOSITE: A series of old family photographs in sepia tones hangs above the bed. The tall Roycroft bookcase was made by Stickley as a centennial piece. The room gets an added touch of liveliness from the leaf motif in the rugs and the colorful fabric of the bed linens.

A Frank Lloyd Wright reading lamp provided the inspiration for the decor of the top-floor master bedroom. (Two guest rooms are on the ground level.) To give the room a cozy, lustrous atmosphere, Maddux emulated Wright's use of metallic paint, applying a liquid copper finish in a series of bold X's. "When the light hits the wall, the brush strokes reflect it in different ways," says Maddux. "And, like all metals, it will achieve a glowing patina with age."

Furniture and needlepoint rugs similar to those used on the main level fill the bedroom. Beside the bed, positioned so that it is the first thing that he sees each morning, hangs a painting of the barns that first attracted Maddux to the site.

A bit of sweat equity and TLC gave this decrepit Fort Worth bungalow a second lease on life. Years of neglect had left the structurally sound house in sorry condition. When Robert Hubatch first set eyes on the tiny 1929 bungalow in the Hillcrest Conservation District, he felt anything but love at first sight for 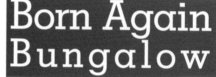 the dwelling. "It was in pretty rough shape," he recalls. "Then," he says, "I looked inside and saw that it was just perfect." For Hubatch, a professional pipe-organ builder, "perfect" meant that the 1,450-square-foot (135sq.m) dwelling "was in fairly good structural shape but needed cosmetic updating." With

New stucco and paint helped to restore the long-neglected bungalow's facade.
The addition of foundation plantings and potted plants made it welcoming.

the enthusiasm of a man who also makes custom furniture, he set about repairing and refinishing ceilings, walls, and oak floors. Hubatch, assisted by friends and family, did all the work: "I saw it as a chance to try out my skills." To spruce up the exterior, gable ends were restuccoed—and repainted along with eaves, window frames, and beams—to harmonize with original brickwork.

Custom ceramic tiles dramatize a once-humdrum fireplace. The easy chair, ottoman, and pedestal table turned an awkward living room corner into a cozy reading nook.

But Hubatch is the first to admit that his skills did not extend to making the best decorating decisions. Enter his friend Gerald Tidwell, a designer for Pier 1. "Robert consulted with me on colors and furnishings," says Tidwell, "to help him maximize the space."

The success of their collaboration is immediately apparent in the living room. Although the area measures 13 3 15 feet (3.9 x 4.5m), the room feels spacious thanks to several decorating tricks—including a color scheme of green for walls and white for trims and ceiling that visually expand the room's boundaries. Another technique to draw attention away from the tight dimensions was to focus on a single element in the room. The obvious choice was the fireplace. To that end, local ceramist Pam Summers created Japanese-style raku tiles; Hubatch capped the new cen-

terpiece with a mantel he designed and built of cherry wood. When the fireplace is not in use, it can be employed as a display area for pottery.

At the far end of the living room, a pair of French doors, original to the house, open to the dining room. Tidwell suggested making the two rooms feel like one larger, continuous space by giving them both the same paint treatment. For the homeowner, the change brought with it another benefit as well. "I had painted the dining room a lighter color, which made it more casual," Hubatch says. "It's a grand room now."

With its understated lines, a cushy, full-size sofa maintains a low profile in the living room.
The French doors lead into the dining room, visually expanding the space.

Befitting such small-scale grandeur, Tidwell hung a brass-accented alabaster chandelier. "It shows," Tidwell explains, "how a somewhat larger lighting fixture in a small-sized room can become a focal point without overpowering it." For Hubatch, however, the most impressive addition was the programmable circuitry that controls the chandelier as well as the recessed ceiling lights in the dining and living rooms. "Each can be adjusted separately on dimmers," he says. "And, there are five different presets to create different moods. It's very dramatic."

ABOVE LEFT: The open structure of the dining table and the metal and wicker chairs keep the small room from feeling cramped. ABOVE RIGHT: In the dining area, shelving on the étagère displays attractive serving pieces, while linens and flatware are stored in baskets.

Equally dramatic is the effect achieved by furnishing the room with wicker-and-metal pieces and combining their clean, crisp styling with a glass-top metal console table that can be used as a buffet. "They have an open, airy feeling that plays well with the room's small space," says Tidwell. Adds his friend and client: "We didn't set out to do a period-type house, but it's funny how well the wicker works with the bungalow style."

Although Robert Hubatch restored most of his bungalow soon after moving in, he held off on its kitchen, which was so cramped that "it wasn't big enough to put any

appliances in." Then a year ago, he says, "I ripped off the end of the house," bumping it out 12½ feet (3.8m) into the backyard to enlarge the bungalow to a still-cozy 1,700 square feet (158sq.m). At the same time, he pulled out all existing cabinetry, save for a built-in hutch that he eventually restored.

The extension added a family room, as well as a new master bath. More importantly, it allowed Hubatch to gain fresh perspective on the cooking space. "I laid out paper cutouts on the floor and pushed the limits a little bit," installing a center cooking island with 3½ foot (1m) clearances from cabinetry. The center island is set off by floor tiles, and baskets on the shelf below the butcher-block counter provide tidy storage for small items.

Hubatch designed and built his own new cherry-wood cabinets, whose natural ruddy finish is echoed by rose granite

New cherry-and-glass doors and a granite counter transformed the formerly decrepit built-in hutch into a showpiece.

counters and two shades of slatelike rose-hued ceramic floor tiles. He borrowed the arched divided-light pattern of the cabinet doors from an old Stickley Arts and Crafts catalog, its period styling just the right look. The curved grid and stainless-steel finishes of the appliances, sink, and fixtures were repeated by local sculptor Damon Now Vaughn in a brushed-steel span that visually bridges the kitchen and family room.

The new family room proved perfect for entertaining, says Hubatch; it "catches any overflow from the kitchen during a party." The wide opening framed with sculptor Vaughn's steelwork ties the two rooms together. Further coordinating the look, here, as in the kitchen, decorator Tidwell chose a "monochromatic look, with different intensities of the same color, to give the illusion of space."

Yet monochromatic does not mean monotonous. The striped upholstery of the sofa, for example, strikes lively harmonies with the muted checkerboard pattern of the earth-toned ceramic floor tiles. A maple television table, designed by Tidwell and built by Hubatch, adds a postmodern touch, repeated in a clock/shelf unit that tucks into a corner and, says Tidwell, "utilizes

OPPOSITE: The newly renovated kitchen offers plenty of room to spread out. An island provides four gas burners, a butcher-block counter, and ample open storage in what was once constricted space. ABOVE: The family room holds the home entertainment equipment, featuring a sleek console that stylishly stores videotapes behind touch-latch doors.

1. **Living room**
2. **Home office**
3. **Bath**
4. **Dining room**
5. **Bedroom**
6. **Kitchen**
7. **Family room**
8. **Master bedroom**
9. **Master bath**

ABOVE: Small metal-based tables rest in front of the striped sofa in the family room, perfect for entertaining. OPPOSITE: Wicker-and-metal furniture and linens in green and rose visually tie the master bedroom to the rest of the house.

a small space by doubling its function." Several small framed pieces of art, grouped together, give the small room the illusion of greater space.

Such attention to small and large details has helped Hubatch transform the ugly duckling he first saw six years ago into a graceful swan. "I wasn't in love with it back then," he admits. "But now, I'm more than in love with it."

Like many

noteworthy homes, this

one began with a scenic location:

Martha's Vineyard in Massachusetts, with a

view stretching northward out across Vineyard

Sound to Woods Hole. Such a prime site, however,

put constraints on the owner's construction bud-

get. "The goal," explains New York City architect

Oliver Cope, "was to build a house

that she could afford with the mort-

gage on her land."

Nevertheless, the owner didn't want to short-

change herself or her frequent weekend guests.

"I wanted something simple, elegant, fun, and not

Architect Oliver Cope's design for this small house hews to a style he calls "Vineyard vernacular," particularly in its exterior composition of peaked roofline, dormer windows, shingles, latticework, and board-and-batten siding. Generous windows take in 270-degree scenery; the first floor's lofty 12-foot (3.6m) height elevates the master bedroom to take in the best view from its balcony.

Multiple entrances to the house—from the living room, the screened porch, and through a stair hall entrance beside the outdoor shower—reinforce a vacation-house informality. The design also allows for future expansion, by adding wings where the stairway and downstairs kitchen/upstairs bath now project from the sides of the house.

intimidating to visitors," she says. She wanted to make the most of the seaside site with budget-conscious touches that would maximize minimal space. With that as their brief, Cope and Falmouth-based contractors Bird, Brown & Company delivered a 1,480-square-foot (137sq.m) house that echoes local architecture and, at the same time, tweaks tradition to gain a greater sense of spaciousness. The house's peaked roofline, dormer windows, and latticework clearly place it in the Vineyard style, yet the 12-foot (3.6m) ceilings on the first floor and the many oversize windows do much to stretch its boundaries and create an expansive feeling.

ABOVE LEFT: Although it measures just 12 × 16 feet (3.6 × 4.8m), the living room feels far larger, thanks to its high ceilings and walls of tall double-hung windows topped by clerestories. With so many windows, the room could have been overly bright, hot, and lacking in privacy when overflow guests slept in it—problems the designer solved by covering the lower windows with Roman shades in a taupe brushed cotton. ABOVE RIGHT: The sofa, also slipcovered in a soft shade of taupe brushed cotton, gains visual interest from piping in a subtly contrasting striped fabric—a pattern also used on the throw cushions.

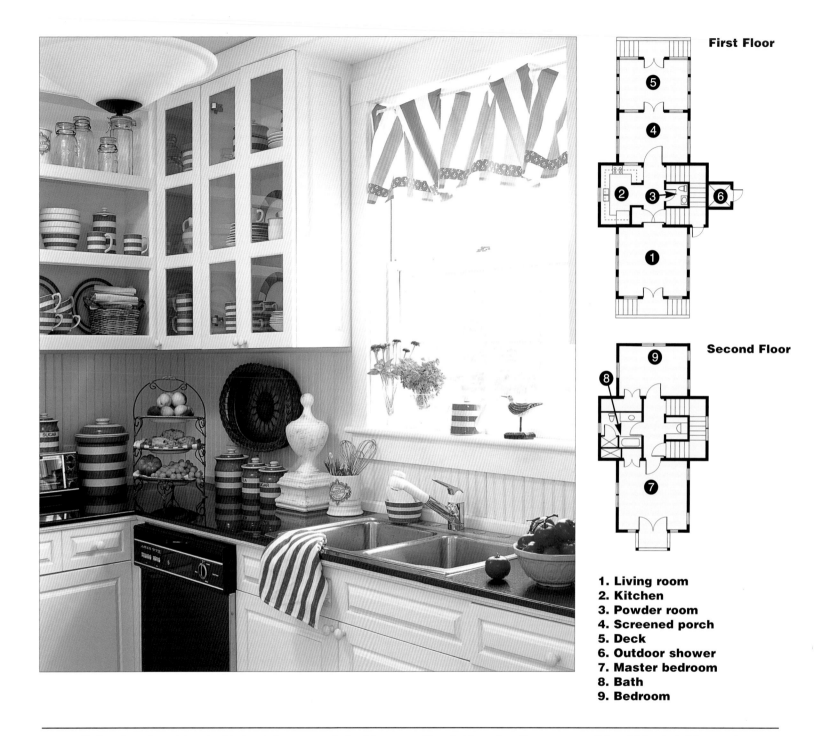

First Floor

Second Floor

1. **Living room**
2. **Kitchen**
3. **Powder room**
4. **Screened porch**
5. **Deck**
6. **Outdoor shower**
7. **Master bedroom**
8. **Bath**
9. **Bedroom**

Painted a crisp white, the kitchen's frame-paneled cabinetry and beaded-board walls restate traditional Martha's Vineyard themes. The blue-and-white stripes of the dishes and storage jars echo the colors of the window valances, which are casually hung by passing the curtain rod back and forth through neatly tailored buttonholes.

The owner then called in Frances W. Halloran, ASID, a Laura Ashley home stylist based in Farmington, Connecticut, to help her "pull together" her eclectic furnishings. The success of the resulting transformation is most immediately evident in the living room, where an old sofa and chairs—grouped around a two-tone table—are custom-slipcovered in green-hued fabrics that pick up the colors of the sea, the surrounding woods, and the owner's favorite fish-themed rug.

In a house that is devoted to graciously accommodating guests who have come to enjoy the outdoors, the kitchen understandably was designed to occupy a minimal space, just 9 ×12 feet (2.7 × 3.6m). But an efficient design arranges major appliances along three walls just steps away from each other and ensures that cooking—an essential element of any weekend entertaining—is accomplished easily and efficiently.

To economize, the homeowner asked a friend to construct the kitchen cabinets for her, and then, she recalls, "his wife and I spray-painted them." The combination of the open shelves and the glass doors on the wall cabinets contributes to the room's bright, open feeling.

Architect Cope's overall house design, in which both kitchen and stairwell jut out some four feet (1.2m) from the sides of the house, provides the small room with ample light from two floor-to-ceiling windows. One of these also functions as a pass-through to the screened porch, where lunch is served alongside potted flowers and window boxes, a cheerful way to bring the outdoors in.

A window serves as a pass-through from the kitchen to a dining area on the house's screened porch. With gardens and woods all around, a variety of colorful fabrics—tulips for the tablecloth, wittily complementing potted flowers and the window box; and summery pink gingham napkins—cheerfully bring the outdoors in and establish a convivial mood for outdoor/indoor entertaining.

Window valances in a blue-and-white striped fabric seem to pull the Vineyard's bright blue skies into the room.

The master bedroom, which features French doors opening onto a balcony, was positioned to enjoy the best water vistas in the house, all the way across to Woods Hole. "It's just lovely to wake up and look at that view," says the homeowner, who adds that on quiet nights she can also hear waves lapping at the nearby shore.

Halloran brought year-round summer to the room by using a flowery chintz fabric strewn with blooms in watercolor shades of blues and pinks for the duvet cover, shams, and curtains. "It's an exuberant, stylized print, but not too busy," she explains. "It feels very cottagey." Avoiding the contrived "overcoordinated ensembles" often seen in summer homes, she mixed other textures and colors—a green-and-white gingham and softly colored print in pink and yellow—for an effect that "feels very fresh, unpretentious, and unstudied." The owner concurs, summing up the look as having a relaxed, breakfast-in-bed, summer pace to it. "It looks like, if I wanted to take credit for it, I could."

Not that she does. In fact, she is eager to give credit where it is due. "Thanks to the architecture and the surroundings and the furniture and fabrics and colors, this house makes everybody feel at home the moment they walk in. The best part is watching other people enjoy it."

ABOVE: At the head of the stairs, just outside the bedroom, built-in bookcases and a desk create a small, open study. Atop the bookcases, oversized newel posts provide visual links to the nearby banister. The result, says the homeowner, is "a creative little corner . . . secluded but without a closed-in feeling." OPPOSITE: With its slanted walls and French doors opening onto a balcony, the bedroom is at once cozy and airy. A summery ambiance is the result of a combination of bed linens in refreshing colors that coordinate with the bedside tablecloth and lampshade, and the bedroom's flowered curtains.

In the best spirit of recycling, this unusual "Best Little House™" was an abandoned nineteenth-century log cabin that was moved from Tennessee to North Carolina. With new furnishings inspired by America's pioneer past, the cabin's full country charm was restored . . . with a modern  twist. "I always wanted a log cabin," says Lee Carter, who happily recalls an old structure used for parties on his father's farm in North Carolina. Ten years ago, when Carter began to put together Southern C's Farm, his own

Set amid the trees and looking out over the Appalachians, the log cabin today looks as if it's always been a part of the Southern C's Farm in Summerfield, North Carolina.

325-acre (131ha) hay and cattle operation in Summerfield, North Carolina, in the Appalachian foothills near the Virginia border, that childhood yearning returned. He eventually found the cabin of his dreams—a two-story, 800-square-foot (74 sq.m) house dating from the 1820s—in the mountains just outside of Knoxville, Tennessee.

Carter had every log of the cabin numbered and disassembled for removal to his farm, where the house was reassembled on a new foundation. There it was joined with another small building that serves as its kitchen, and given three new fieldstone fireplaces.

A stickler for authenticity, Carter and local restoration experts combed the countryside for such period details as original hand-blown window panes, handmade rose-head nails, and wide-plank pine flooring to give the cabin authentic accents. Furnishing the cabin, however, presented a challenge, since Carter planned to rent it out as an idyllic site for

ABOVE: Rocking chairs situated on the long front porch invite guests to take their ease and sip lemonade.
OPPOSITE: With log walls, fieldstone fireplace, and beamed ceiling, even a small log cabin such as this can feel massive, so Mary Emmerling selected substantial furniture. In the living room, that includes a leather sofa, wing chairs in a blue-and-white plaid, and an oak cocktail table. Using a variety of accessories with bright colors and lively textures and patterns—among them a red-and-white-striped woven rug—Emmerling also effectively countered the room's inherent darkness.

Original siding from another log cabin panels the bedroom ceiling. Flanking the massive bed are a table and nightstand. The blue-and-white color scheme used so effectively in the public rooms is continued here in the bed linens and rugs.

The bedroom may well be the most inviting space of all. Generously proportioned, the room occupies the entire second floor of the cabin, its ceiling rising high to the roofline. What's more, it features a nine-pane picture window, a true extravagance for its era, which Carter maximized by siting the house so the window faces westward to behold breathtaking Appalachian sunsets over beautiful pastures.

Emmerling boldly made the most of the bedroom's dimensions by making its centerpiece a queen-sized bed, a sizable piece that makes Carter think of the kinds of family heirlooms Swedish or German settlers might have brought with them from the Old

Country. "Using a really big piece of furniture like that," adds Emmerling, "gives the room some oomph." Setting it at an angle adds spatial interest and allows one to appreciate not only the view but also the fireplace, which sits directly opposite the foot of the bed.

Here, once more, Emmerling brought the crisp, refreshing blue colors of bright skies into what could have been a gloomy interior by accessorizing the bedroom in blue and white (accented with a bold touch of red). The overall effect she achieved is so welcoming, so comforting, that one can easily understand Carter when he admits, "All my life, I lived in the city and always traveled to the country; but now that I live in the country, I am definitely reluctant to travel back to the city."

A model log cabin sits atop a rustic chest, while the wall behind it holds an artist's rendition of a country house.

James M. O'Connor
teaches a class at UCLA
titled "Designing a Small House:
An American Dream." The Santa Monica
house that he and his wife, fellow architect
Sue O'Brien, designed for themselves and their
two young sons could easily serve as the course

textbook. Born in Ireland but now
Americans, the two claim their
design philosophy was influenced
by Japanese minimalism and the
vibrant colors of Mexico. They also acknowledge
a debt to late artist Richard Diebenkorn, who
lived in the same Ocean Park neighborhood, and
whose luminous landscapes inspired many of the

Yellow stucco clads the façade of the 1,850-square-foot (172sq.m) house designed by James M. O'Connor and Sue O'Brien.

colors that the couple use in their house to trick the eye into thinking the space is larger than it actually is. Rounding off the multinational influences, the 1,850-square-foot (172sq.m) house also reveals a debt to Europe in its lemon yellow stucco façade. The L-shaped house is sited in the center of its narrow lot. (A tiny, pre-existing 1940s bungalow occupies the front of the lot, and is rented out. Some day, it may link up with the new house as a family room or office.) A formal European-style garden leads from the street to a slate courtyard; to the rear is what O'Brien calls her rose-filled "wild Irish garden."

"Perceived space is important in a small house," says O'Connor, explaining how landscape is crucial to the design of a house. "In a California courtyard house, the outside is an extension of the house itself. It's what the Japanese call 'borrowed space.'" For example, the living room window, placed high on the fireplace wall, reveals an inviting ocean vista from the stairwell.

ABOVE: Streamlined furniture designed by Heywood-Wakefield in the 1940s recalls the sophistication of an earlier era yet suits the house's contemporary mood and small scale. OPPOSITE: The living room's tall French doors extend the room by opening it to the outdoors, while the lush use of color vividly stresses the importance of the hearth.

A galley-style kitchen is separated from the dining area by a waist-high counter. In the dining area, the
Heywood-Wakefield table and chairs set a mood that is sleek yet comfortable.

O'Connor and O'Brien punched up square footage with expanded volumes. The living room's ceiling stretches 12 feet (3.6m) high, but the kitchen and dining room sacrifice two feet (60cm) to accommodate plumbing beneath the floors. The stairwell rises dramatically the full 25-foot (7.6m) height of the house. Ceilings on the upper floor extend to the roofline.

ABOVE LEFT: The sink is set into the counter that separates kitchen from dining area. On the opposite wall of the kitchen, another counter stretches the full length of the room, offering plenty of work space. A door leads from the kitchen into the backyard garden. ABOVE RIGHT: A dramatic maple stairway rises 25 feet (7.6m), its effect heightened by tricolored walls with display niches. The rug adds more subtle hues.

It is the use of color, however, that defines the space. "Color allows you to get a lot of richness out of something modest," says O'Connor. The couple tried out dozens of hues. All ceilings are painted shell white, while all of the floors on the ground level are maple strip, to serve as a consistent frame for the vertical planes of color. The paint on the walls

Continuing the theme of vivid color contrasting with blond streamlined furniture, the master suite features a wall of vibrant blueberry behind the bed.

First Floor

Second Floor

1. Living room
2. Bath
3. Study/Bedroom
4. Dining room
5. Kitchen
6. Studio
7. Bedroom
8. Master bedroom
9. Master bath
10. Study

gives each room its own identity, and each color choice works on several levels. For example, the living room's "Auburn" establishes the primacy of the hearth and heightens the effect of southern light falling on the west-facing wall. Off the master bedroom, walls change hue as you move through the book-lined library to the study. "Bachelor Button" on the staircase wall evokes the color of the sky, its shade modified by a skylight over the landing. "When light reacts with color, it vibrates and changes," notes O'Connor, who was inspired by artist Tina Beebe's use of light and color.

Equally eye-catching streamlined furniture complements the rooms' sleek lines and fresh colors. Originally designed in the 1940s and 1950s, the pieces have been re-created in an array of upholstery fabrics. "What I like about the furniture," says O'Connor, "is that it is rich and modern, like the house." The openness of the pieces' wood frames also means they do not appear to take up a lot of space, a key consideration in small quarters.

Located off the master bedroom, the study is reached through a book-lined library. The walls change hue as vertical planes shift.

This 1,325-square-foot (123sq.m) home, located on a modest-size lot in Greensboro, North Carolina, is a model of creative renovation. The 1927 "Southern bungalow" had been virtually untouched for years, which meant that its vintage style was nicely preserved. It also meant many nights and weekends of work for Mark Weppner, owner and mastermind  of the most recent renovation, who peeled off paint and roofing to bring the little one-story cottage back to life. Weppner also restored some exterior details—which had lost historical accuracy in earlier renovations—to their original form. The face-lift produced a house of timeless charm.

Situated on a side street in Greensboro, North Carolina, the charmingly landscaped house is nestled among the trees.

"What attracted me to the house was its windows," says Weppner. "There are so many windows I have almost no wall to hang a picture on. But there's wonderful morning sun and plenty of shade when the weather is hot. And the house is neatly tucked away amid landscaping, like a country cottage."

The influence of the Arts and Crafts movement is readily apparent in the living room's comfortable furniture and accessories. Levolor blinds filter sunlight.

Weppner kept period details throughout the house—such as the original solid oak flooring and white-painted brick fireplace in the living room—but augmented them with new touches like the 7½ inch (19cm) crown moldings, which "give the walls a finished look," says the homeowner. A collector, Weppner wanted to combine old pieces he's gathered with new ones. The new furniture in the living room and throughout the house, comes from a collection inspired by the Arts and Crafts movement in general and North Carolina art pottery in particular, and provides a sense of American tradition and simple, handcrafted styling.

To open the dining room to the kitchen, Weppner created a well-positioned pass-through. "I had it cut out and trimmed to match the size and proportions of the windows," he explains. The dining room's tall windows and 9½-foot (2.8m) ceiling are accentuated by

the high backs of the armchairs and bench, pulled up to the rectangular dining table. The distinctive fretwork pattern visually links the living room's entertainment center with the dining room chair backs and buffet base doors.

The scale of the furniture certainly suits the lofty spaces in this house, as does that of the kitchen's custom cabinets. Their tall, narrow doors have an Arts and Crafts look that is underscored by brass drawer pulls. Also new is the parquet wood flooring. The backsplashes as well as the countertops are made of laminate designed to look like stone. As throughout the house, an abundance of windows lights the room. When Weppner prepares

In the dining room, the pass-through makes an architectural statement, echoing the window and door moldings. The green and gold rug and softly hued walls provide a perfect setting for the Arts and Crafts-style furniture.

food at the kitchen's 6-foot (1.8m) -long peninsula, he faces a wall of eight rear windows that flood the kitchen with daylight and provide him with lush views of his beautifully landscaped backyard.

Master bedroom walls and ceiling are painted in a shade of green that, says Mark Weppner, "mimics the leaf tone of the huge, shade-producing magnolia tree outside, just beyond the window." Here, blinds are combined with loop-top draperies to provide greater privacy and light control.

In helping Weppner furnish his cottage, located in the historic Fisher Park district of Greensboro, designer Michael Foster was undaunted by the rooms' compact dimensions. By using fewer but larger-scaled pieces, he was able to provide needed storage without crowding

the room with a miscellany of smaller furnishings. Foster selected a massive panel bed and door chest; they dominate the master bedroom without overwhelming the space. To soften the impact of so much grained wood, Foster chose inviting bed coverings, including throw and sheets plus shams, comforter, bedskirt, and decorative pillows, and a Tibetan carpet.

Although his three-bedroom house is small, with a very basic floor plan, Weppner insists that privacy is not lacking anywhere. There is a guest bath, but the master bath serves two bedrooms. No problem. Shutting one hall door gives his own room the serenity he always hoped his home would have, despite the size and number of windows.

In the kitchen, oversize custom-designed cabinets and plentiful drawers and cupboards provide storage. The pass-through to the dining area is set above the sink, allowing for easy access.

"The house was built for a newlywed couple from Florida," he recalls. "According to local legend, the bride said that the only way she would move 'north' was if she could have a magnolia tree—and a house with a lot of windows. The magnolia is about 40 feet (12.1m) tall today, and the windows are just as they were originally. By painting the woodwork white, I could give them the emphasis they deserve."

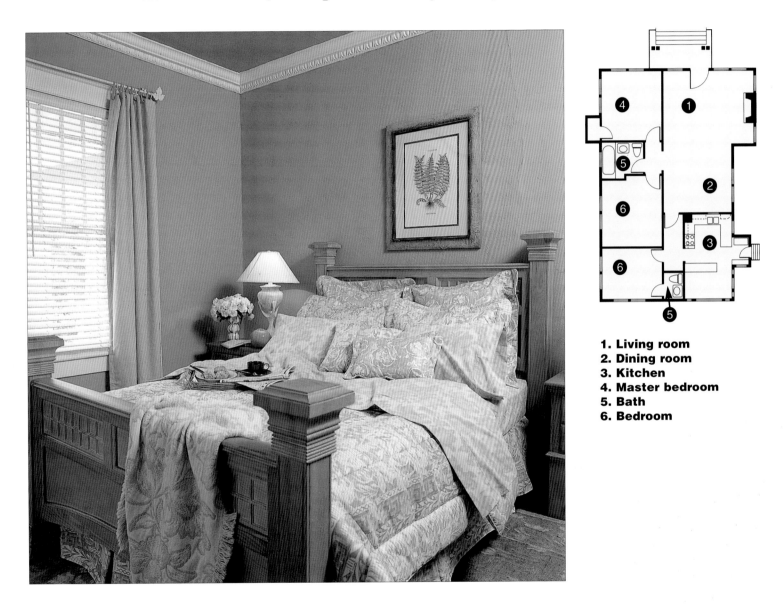

1. Living room
2. Dining room
3. Kitchen
4. Master bedroom
5. Bath
6. Bedroom

Furnished with an impressive wooden bed, the master suite features soothing green paint and patterned bed coverings. The overall effect is inviting and comfortable.

A native Los Angeleno and distant relative of the impresario with whom he shares his name, Billy Rose is also in the entertainment business. After a brief stint as a performer, he studied law and is now a partner in a firm that specializes in entertainment law. Rose admits that entertaining is in his blood in other ways as well. "I often

invite three or four hundred people over for a wine tasting," he tosses off. What makes this statement all the more remarkable is that the house in which he's doing this entertaining is just 1,800 square feet (167sq.m).

This modest Spanish Revival house in Los Angeles was built in 1923. Knocking down interior walls and renovating a previous addition enlarged the small rooms and added a bathroom, increasing the living space significantly.

After purchasing the 1923 Spanish Revival house in 1990, Rose worked with architect Peter A. DiSabatino to "make the place livable," that is, to remodel the kitchen, and "give the house a greater sense of spaciousness." To this end, they knocked out walls to transform the original kitchen, breakfast room, and utility room into a single space suitable for both cooking and socializing. In phase two, five years later, architect Chris Callett stepped in, removing what Rose refers to as a "trailer park extension" off the bedroom, incorporating the space into the master bedroom and adding another bathroom.

Around this time, interior designer Kelly Wearstler, a former film industry set designer, joined the team. "Billy wanted a contemporary feel and a fun atmosphere," she recalls. "But instead of new furniture that might be out of style in five years, I suggested we go with pieces that will stand the test of time." Thus began the seven-month-long odyssey of assembling furnishings that serve as a metaphor for the decorative arts of the first half of the twentieth century. In keeping with classics like original Heywood-Wakefield tables and chairs from the 1940s and 1950s are Murano glass, California art pottery, and Rose's own collection of original Billy Rose memorabilia.

"I didn't want to use just 1950s pieces," notes Wearstler, "because the look can be too kitschy. So I pulled things from different decades." The resulting eclectic environment is masculine yet whimsical, perfectly suited to her client's expansive personality. "Kelly introduced me to the clean and organic lines of moderne furniture by the likes of Le Corbusier and Eames," notes Rose, who joined her in many of the forays to antique shops, swap meets, flea markets, and tag sales. Summing up the collaboration, the homeowner comments, "She macroed and I microed."

One piece he particularly fell in love with was the vintage Heywood-Wakefield wishbone dining table, which became the catalyst for the room's design scheme. "It was obvious that nothing that I had worked with it." Around the blond table, Wearstler placed teak dining chairs by Danish artisan Hans Wegner, a find of which she is especially proud: "These days, it's hard to find six of anything." In addition to its graceful lines, the table is eminently suited to Rose's social life. With several leaves, it can

Placing seating on the diagonal makes the living room look larger. The organic forms typical of the "moderne" style popular during the 1930s mix with later furniture, including a 1940s Heywood-Wakefield end table and a 1950s marble coffee table, to form an eclectic, stylish result.

Given a makeover

by a clothing retailer and

his family, this once-ramshackle

Long Island house now boasts a gabled

second story, an airy all-weather porch,

and a new sheltered entry—all in approximately

2,000 square feet (180sq.m).

While searching for a summer

house on eastern Long Island, Jay

and Joan McLaughlin came across the little place

with a gently sloping lawn and a surround of lush

trees. Trouble was, it was dilapidated and cramped,

and had no relationship to the outdoors. A consul-

tation with architect Douglas E. Larson of Bell

Larson Architects & Planners in New York City

In remodeling the original house, the owners opted for lots of outdoor rooms, including a small front porch, an L-shaped back deck, and the indoor-outdoor Florida room. To increase the usable space on the second floor, a series of gables topped the house, adding charm as well.

reassured the couple that the house had good bones and could be revamped for easy living. Larson did just that, adding an all-weather porch to the lawn side of the house, outfitting the unfinished attic with two bedrooms and a bath, and reconfiguring the first-floor rooms. Although the renovation added only about 900 square feet (81sq.m), it

In the airy, multipurpose Florida room, the McLaughlins eat breakfast, gather for family dinners, or curl up by the Robert Abbey lamps with a book on rainy afternoons. The dining chairs display the fine detailing of the British Colonial furniture that inspired the style.

transformed the little house. There is now plenty of casual, sun-splashed space for Joan, Jay, their three children, and their weekend guests.

The most significant change made during the remodeling was the addition of the indoor-outdoor porch, which increased living space by 350 square feet (31.5sq.m). In spite of its compact size, it quickly became a sort of Florida room that forms the heart of this summer house. In cooler months, sliding doors make the room a cozy place to be as well. A deep sofa, cushy armchairs, and plump pillows, all upholstered in crisp blue and white, offer

luxurious comfort; ottomans double as coffee tables. The rich mahogany cabinet and end table play up the warm wood tones of the floor, and serve to anchor the room.

Once structural remodeling was sorted out, Jay turned to his brother Kevin for design assistance. The two men have been co-owners of the J. McLaughlin Clothing Collection for many years, but recently Kevin added furniture design to his list of talents. His new line was just right for the relaxed elegance Joan and Jay wanted.

The kitchen was not enlarged, but its haphazard existing layout was completely renovated to make it efficient and to allow several cooks to work comfortably together to produce an informal meal. The spruced-up space has an appropriately casual air and its decor reflects the interests of this seafaring family. "The owners wanted to do this room fairly inexpensively," says Larson, "so we bought unfinished cabinets from a home center, gave them a couple of coats of white paint, and added bright-red hardware."

The McLaughlins preside over an occasional formal dinner party in the casually elegant dining room. A mahogany-framed mirror hangs above the Somerset sideboard. The seats of the slat-back chairs are covered in practical pinstriped denim; yellow plaid curtains made from sheets add a sunny feeling.

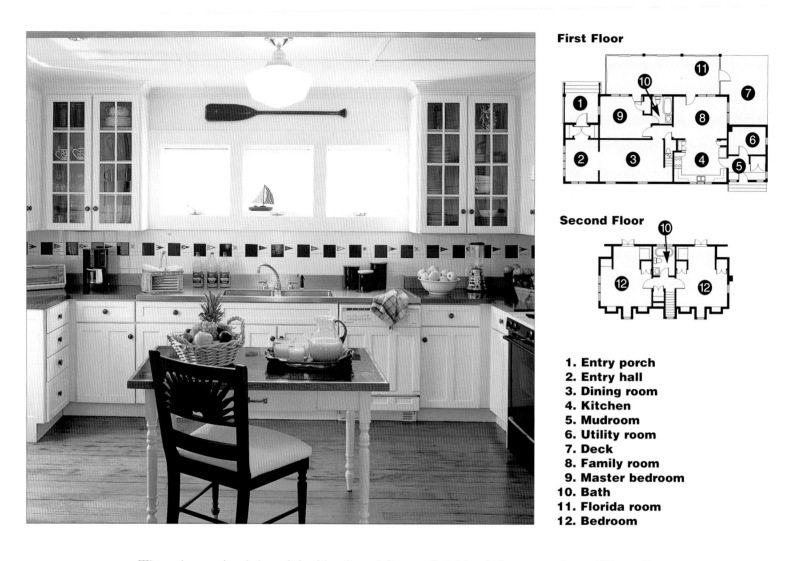

First Floor

Second Floor

1. **Entry porch**
2. **Entry hall**
3. **Dining room**
4. **Kitchen**
5. **Mudroom**
6. **Utility room**
7. **Deck**
8. **Family room**
9. **Master bedroom**
10. **Bath**
11. **Florida room**
12. **Bedroom**

They also retained the original hardwood floor, refinishing it for a new sheen. The striking backsplash is made up of navy blue ceramic tiles on a white ground, interspersed with decorative pieces depicting signal flags from various yacht clubs. "Someone gave the tiles to Kevin as a gift," says Jay McLaughlin, "and we all worked on the design to make it really pop."

In the kitchen, the countertops and table are clad with mahogany; white paint and red accents create a bright, cheery feeling. A Palmetto side chair adds a classic touch.

To create a master suite on the first floor, Larson closed off public access to the existing bath, and made it part of the bedroom, which had adjoined it. He beefed up privacy by giving the bedroom its own door to the new entry porch at the side of the house. For guest use, he then tucked a small powder room under the flight of stairs that led to the attic, an ingenious use of normally wasted space.

The second floor was formerly an unfinished attic. Adding three gables improved the look of the exterior, giving it an interesting façade for the lawn view. The gables also created headroom for the children's sleeping quarters and allowed the inclusion of a bath. The new bedrooms are compact and cozy and "fabulous," says Jay McLaughlin, "sort of like ships' cabins." McLaughlin, in fact, thinks the whole house is fabulous. "It really is a great place," he says. "There are no excesses; everything is utilized. It's very functional and has a comfortable lived-in feeling that's perfect for our family."

ABOVE LEFT: The handy mudroom has a jaunty painted floor. The benches and wicker table are antiques.
ABOVE RIGHT: The master bedroom sports a queen-size sleigh bed. Cheerful yellow-and-white curtains fashioned from sheets hang on wooden rods with shell finials. The shell motif is repeated in the rug's border.

This three-story clapboard guest house in Florida's Seaside community is a raffish companion to the main house, which recalls the staid mansions of Charleston, South Carolina. Houses that are built in the planned community of Seaside, Florida, must conform in style to particular codes that relate

to historically significant places, says New Haven, Connecticut, architect Robert Orr. That explains the main source of inspiration for this two-dwelling vacation home. Situated on a lot in the "Charleston" section of Seaside, the main

Designed to be wholly separate from the main house, the metal-roofed guest house has its own style.
It is physically linked to the main house via a two-story porch and a pergola.

Since the house is sited on the western edge of the Seaside community, the ground-floor bedroom was given a slightly Western theme. Pegs beneath the wrap-around hat shelf are convenient for hanging wet swimwear and lobster pot buoys, but a cowpoke could hang his hat there, too. Dominating this tiny space is an iron bed found at a going-out-of-business sale and embellished. To give this new bed a period charm, a pediment was added to the headboard and turned-wood finials were put on each post. To further "age" the frame, it was painted with five coats of paint that are all crackled so they peel back and reveal the coats below. Providing still more character to the bedroom, the plywood floor and all the woodwork are ebony-stained then varnished to reveal the grain of the wood peeking through.

The top-floor bedroom—accessible only via a set of stairs from the second floor—has a ski-lodge theme. A ski house in Florida? "Looking out of the windows, I saw all those peaked silver metal roofs, and they reminded me of snow-covered mountain peaks," the owner recalls. So he transported a collection of old skis and snowshoes from his winter home and hung them on the walls. A sled sits atop the ceiling of the adjacent bathroom and, appropriately, a sleigh bed is the room's centerpiece. The result is a delightful anachronism: beyond the metal "mountain peaks" is the Gulf of Mexico, sparkling in the sunlight.

The bedroom on the top floor, though small in square footage, nevertheless seems spacious thanks to the high ceilings. Hat shelves lining the walls feature a row of pegs—a storage bonus.

In the ground-floor bedroom, colorful bed linens accent the painted antique bed. A doorway leads out to the porch, screened by curtains made from sheets that coordinate with the bed linens.

Tile ceramics for fireplace: Pam Summers
Metal console table: Medicci
Kitchen: Ceramic floor tiles: American Marazzi
    Appliance: KitchenAid
    Sink: Franke
    Metalwork: Damon Vaughn

ISLAND RETREAT: PP. 94-101
PHOTOGRAPHER: ERIC ROTH (617) 338-5358
Architect: Oliver Cope (212) 727-1225
Designer: Frances W. Halloran, ASID (203) 521-8967
Stylist: Michael Foster (212) 874-0066
Reader Service for all Laura Ashley products and Home Styling Service: (800) 367-2000
Vicki Enteen, Publicity Manager for Laura Ashley's Home Furnishings (212) 735-5000
Frances W. Halloran, ASID, Home Stylist for Laura Ashley (203) 521-8967
Fabrics on furniture and pillows, bed linens, fabric on bedroom draperies, rug in bedroom, napkin on bed tray, lamps in bedroom, tableround in bedroom all from Laura Ashley
Wood pieces of furniture all from Nichols & Stone
Living room: Horizontally-striped pillow with white trimming, pillow on rattan chair: Manderley
    Coffee Table: Nichols & Stone
    Painted terra cotta flower pots, white washed finials: Ballard Designs
    Throw: Faribo
    Wicker plant stand: Palecek
Study: Chair: Nichols & Stone
    Computer and keyboard: Compaq
    Trophies, pencil holders, bird houses, pots: Ballard Designs
    Basket with handle, wire basket, wooden bird: Palecek
    Photo album: Exposures
Bedroom: Basket/tray: Palecek
    Glass vase, bird house, flowered bowl, plaid pillow: Ballard Designs
    Bed: Crate & Barrell
    Teacup and saucer and teapot: Cuthbertson Imports
Kitchen: All China: Cuthberson Imports, T.G. Green through Pamela Winterfield Gifts
    White finials: Ballard Designs
    Red and white striped dishtowel, folded dishtowels on top of basket on wall cabinet: Tag
    Wire plate stand on counter, sunflower tray, wooden bird: Palecek
    Bead Board (wainscoting): Georgia Pacific
Exterior: Floor plants: Steve Stankiewicz

CABIN COMEBACK: PP. 102-109
PHOTOGRAPHER: DOUGLAS KENNEDY
Stylist: Mary Emmerling
Porch: Rocking chairs: Mary Emmerling's American Country West Collection from Lexington Glasses: Wolfman-Gold & Good Company
    "House" end table: GuildMaster's Best of Mary Emmerling Collection
    Accessories: Clay City

Living room: Lone Star sofa, wing chairs, cocktail table: Mary Emmerling's American Country West Collection from Lexington
    Rug: Woodard & Greenstein
    Accessories: GuildMaster, Lady Slipper Designs
Kitchen: Table, side chairs: Mary Emmerling's American Country West Collection from Lexington
    Dinnerware: Mesa International
    Gingham napkins: Wolfman-Gold & Good
    Casseroles and crockery: Clay City Pottery
    Print: GuildMaster
Bedroom: Bed, table, nightstand: Mary Emmerling's American Country West Collection from Lexington
    Bed linens: Springmaid
    Rugs: Woodard & Greenstein
    Leather pillow, Beaver Weathervane, Pine Tree Sconces, and "Appliqué Crib Quilt": Guild Master
    Chest: Lexington
    Accessories: Clay City, Lady Slipper Designs

PENCHANT FOR DESIGN: PP. 5, 110-117
PHOTOGRAPHER: GREY CRAWFORD
Photographer's Rep: Beate Works Management & Production
Stylist: Charles Riley
Porch: All chairs: Homeowner's Collection
Living Room: All furniture: Heywood-Wakefield
    Rug: David Shaw Nicholls
    Tiki lamp, ceramics, large vase, shallow DWP bowl: Gallery of Functional Art
    Pillows on chairs, pillow on corner of sofa, birdcage: Hollyhock
    White pillow on corner of sofa, pink and red striped pillow: Manderley
    All other accessories: Homeowner's Collection
Stairs area: Rug: David Shaw Nicholls
    Chairs: Heywood-Wakefield
    Guitar and vases: Homeowner's Collection
Home Office: Lamp on desk, basket in red and blue: Gallery of Functional Art
    Basket on floor: Hollyhock
    All other: Homeowner's Collection
Bedroom: All furniture: Heywood-Wakefield
    Two pillows on bed: Manderley
    Bedding: WAMSUTTA
    Telechron clock: Once Upon A Table
    Ornament on chest: Hollyhock
    All other: Homeowner's Collection
Kitchen Table and chairs: Heywood-Wakefield
    Prints on wall, green basket, green tray: Hollyhock
Dinnerware: plates, cups, bowls, bakelite handle forks and knives, juice glasses, glass juice pitcher, ice pail, serving bowl, teapot, green mixing bowl, green egg cups, rolling pin, coffee pot, drink mixer, toaster oven, tea and coffee servers, coffee urn, chrome cocktail shaker, two-tier silver tray: Once Upon A Table

PAST MADE PERFECT: PP. 1, 118-123
PHOTOGRAPHER: DEBORAH MAZZOLENI
Designer: Michael Foster
All Furniture: American Drew Seagrove Collection
Bedding, Curtains, Curtain Rods, Throws: Croscill
Window Blinds: Levolor
Rugs: Michaelian & Kohlberg
Paint for master bedroom, living room, dining room: The Glidden Company & ICI Paints
Front of house: Table, chairs: Vance Kitira
    Glass coolers: Mesa International
Living room: Lamps: Robert Abbey
    Kilim pillows on sofa: Eastern Accents
    Rectangular shaped pillow in middle of sofa: What a Clever Girl!
    Beige pillow, two sofas: Homeowner's Collection
    Candle: Tag
    Ivy ball topiary in maple syrup bucket, 18th century botanical engraving, 1880 architectural star, 1920 architectural star, Arts & Crafts rocker, iron fragment table with glass top, twig, painted side table: The Farmer's Wife
    Large botanical print, three botanical prints on wall: GuildMaster
    Two vases on mantle, small bowl on coffee table, white crackle raku vase: Turn & Burn Pottery
    Large blue bowl: Tom Gray Pottery
    Rust bowl: Wild Rose Pottery
    Decorative pillow inserts: DuPont Sleep Products
    Iron basket on entertainment center: Import Specialists
    Iron footed urn: Robert Abbey
    Moldings: Ornamental Moldings
Bedroom: Lamp: Robert Abbey
    Botanical print: GuildMaster
    Pillow inserts: DuPont Sleep Products
    Serving tray: Bance Kitira
    Cup and saucer: "Craftworks" by Lindt-Stymeist Designs, designed by John Stymeist
    White and turquoise vases: Turn & Burn Pottery
    Large flower vase: Tom Gray pottery
    Woodash vase: Wild Rose Pottery
    Jar with lid: DirtWorks Pottery
    Cast iron grate, "Wagon Wheel" window: The Farmer's Wife
Dining room: Aqua blue raku vase: Turn & Burn Pottery
    Small appliances: Krups
    Hanging lamp: Stiffel
    Standing lamp: Robert Abbey
Hutch: (top shelf left) Vase with ash glaze, glazed bottle, (top shelf right) glazed, fluted bottle, (bottom shelf left) vase, shallow bowl with tracing, (bottom shelf right) small vase with ash glaze, two goblets with ash glaze, (middle shelf left) glazed vase: Tom Gray Pottery (bottom shelf) Small salt glaze bowl, (second shelf right) white crackle raku vase, (left side) aqua blue raku vase: Turn & Burn Pottery
    "Candlesticks" teapots: DirtWorks Pottery

Woodash vase: Wild Rose Pottery
    Two handle urn: David Stuempfle Pottery from the DirtWorks Collection

CONTEMPORARY CLASSIC: PP. 124-129
PHOTOGRAPHER: GREY CRAWFORD
Stylist: Charles Riley
Interior Designer: Kelly Wearstler
Architects: Peter A. DiSabatino and Chris Calatt
Living Room: Printed pillow on chair: Manderley
    End table: Heywood-Wakefield
    Pottery: Bauer, McCoy, and Hall
Dining room: Table: Heywood-Wakefield
    Chairs: Hans Wegner
Bedroom: Printed pillow on bed: Manderley
    Dresser/buffet, bedside tables: Heywood-Wakefield
    Bed: Modernica

FASHION COMES HOME: PP. 130-135
PHOTOGRAPHER: KARI HAAVISTO
Designer: Michael Foster
Porch: Furniture: Bermuda Run by J. McLaughlin for Bassett, available through the Design Store at the Door Store.
    Tablecloth: Made of Fortrel and cotton sheets by Alexander Julian for Dan River
    Rug, placemat: Import Specialists
    Accessories: Libbey, Palecek.
Dining Room: Accessories: Libbey, Vietri, Import Specialists, Palecek;
    Lamps: Robert Abbey.
    Furniture: Bermuda Run for Bassett at the Door Store
Sun Porch: Sailboat: The Design Store at the Door Store.
Kitchen: Tea Kettle: Moller Design;
    Dishtowel: Tag; Towels: Martex;
    Accessories: Palecek, Chantal.
Master Bedroom: Bed linens and curtains (made from Fortrel and cotton sheets): Alexander Julian for Dan River
    Iron Bench: Hildreth's
    Throws, Rug: Import Specialists
    Accessories: Palecek.

SOUTHERN COMFORT WITH MODERN STYLE: PP. 136-141
PHOTOGRAPHER: CHRIS LITTLE
Designer: Michael Foster
Living room: Furniture and accessories: Pier 1 Imports
    Curtains and slipcovers: Made from sheets by Liz at Home/Liz Claiborne #11UP3C
Dining table: Pier 1 Imports.
Ground-floor bedroom: Armchair and table: Pier 1 Imports
    Sheets and towels: Liz at Home/Liz Claiborne
Top-floor bedroom: Bed linens: Liz at Home/Liz Claiborne